A FIRST LOOK AT HISTORY

Pirates

by Brian Williams

Consultant: Richard Platt

GARETH**STEVENS**
GS
PUBLISHING
A WRC Media Company

Please visit our web site at: www.garethstevens.com
For a free color catalog describing Gareth Stevens Publishing's
list of high-quality books and multimedia programs, call
1-800-542-2595 (USA) or 1-800-387-3178 (Canada).
Gareth Stevens Publishing's fax: (414) 332-3567.

Library of Congress Cataloging-in-Publication Data available upon request
from publisher. Fax (414) 336-0157 for the attention of the Publishing
Records Department.

ISBN 0-8368-4529-3

This edition first published in 2005 by
Gareth Stevens Publishing
A WRC Media Company
330 West Olive Street, Suite 100
Milwaukee, Wisconsin 53212 USA

This U.S. edition copyright © 2005 by Gareth Stevens, Inc.
Original edition copyright © 2004 by ticktock Entertainment Ltd.
First published in Great Britain in 2005 by ticktock Media Ltd.,
Unit 2, Orchard Business Centre, North Farm Road, Tunbridge
Wells, Kent, TN2 3XF, United Kingdom.

Gareth Stevens series editor: Dorothy L. Gibbs
Gareth Stevens art direction: Tammy West

Picture credits (t=top, b=bottom, c=center, l=left, r=right)
AKG: 5br. Album Archivo Fotografico: 2-3, 4, 5tl, 8-9, 9tl, 10-11,
12tl, 14-15. Corbis: 6, 7tr, 20-21. e.t. Archive: 7bl. Heritage Image
Partnership: 7tl (The British Library), 19br (The British Museum).
Mary Evans Picture Library: 7br. National Maritime Museum: 9tr,
13l, 13br, 17cr, 21tl, 22l, 22-23, 23cr. Royal Armouries: 15cr.
Ticktock: 1, 5tr, 5cr, 9br, 11r (all), 12b, 13tr, 13cr, 15tr, 15br,
16-17, 17tr, 17br, 19tr, 21r (both), 23tr, 23br.

Every effort has been made to trace the copyright holders for the
photos used in this book. The publisher apologizes, in advance, for
any unintentional omissions and would be pleased to insert appropriate
acknowledgments in any subsequent edition of this publication.

Printed in the United States of America

1 2 3 4 5 6 7 8 9 09 08 07 06 05

Contents

Words in the glossary are printed in **boldface** type the first time they appear in the text.

Meet the Pirates

Pirates are robbers who sail the seas in search of treasure. There have been pirates throughout history, but the most famous pirates date back to long ago. About three hundred years ago, lots of pirates sailed the seas. There were even women pirates!

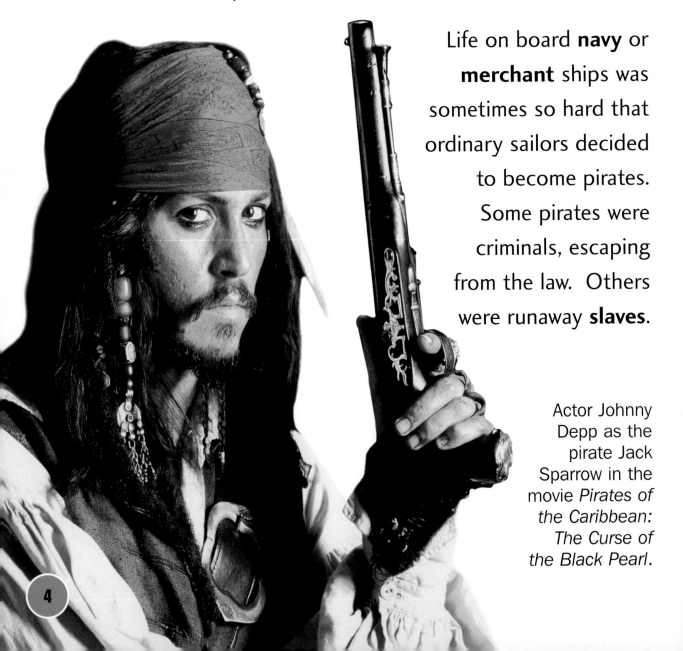

Life on board **navy** or **merchant** ships was sometimes so hard that ordinary sailors decided to become pirates. Some pirates were criminals, escaping from the law. Others were runaway **slaves**.

Actor Johnny Depp as the pirate Jack Sparrow in the movie *Pirates of the Caribbean: The Curse of the Black Pearl*.

A scene from the pirate movie *Cutthroat Island*.

Pirates from the **Caribbean** were called buccaneers. Pirates who sailed the Mediterranean Sea were known as corsairs.

A privateer was a pirate who worked for a country's government. Privateers attacked ships that belonged to enemy countries.

Famous Pirates

A life spent stealing treasure might sound exciting, but the lives of many pirates came to a **gruesome** end.

The famous pirate Blackbeard, whose real name was Edward Teach, attacked ships in the Caribbean. His evil ways terrified not only sailors but also his own crew. When Blackbeard was cornered by the British Navy, in 1718, it took five gunshots and twenty **cutlass** slashes to kill him.

Welshman Bartholomew Roberts, who was known as Black Bart, was one of the most successful pirates who ever lived. He captured more than four hundred ships in his lifetime.

Captain William Kidd started out hunting pirates for the government of England, but his crew of **cutthroats** turned him into a pirate. In the end, Kidd was hanged for **piracy**.

Women Pirates

Mary Read was a woman who dressed up as a man and became a famous British pirate.

Anne Bonny also disguised herself as a man to be a pirate. She sailed with Mary Read in the Caribbean.

When they were captured, Read and Bonny escaped hanging because they were **pregnant**.

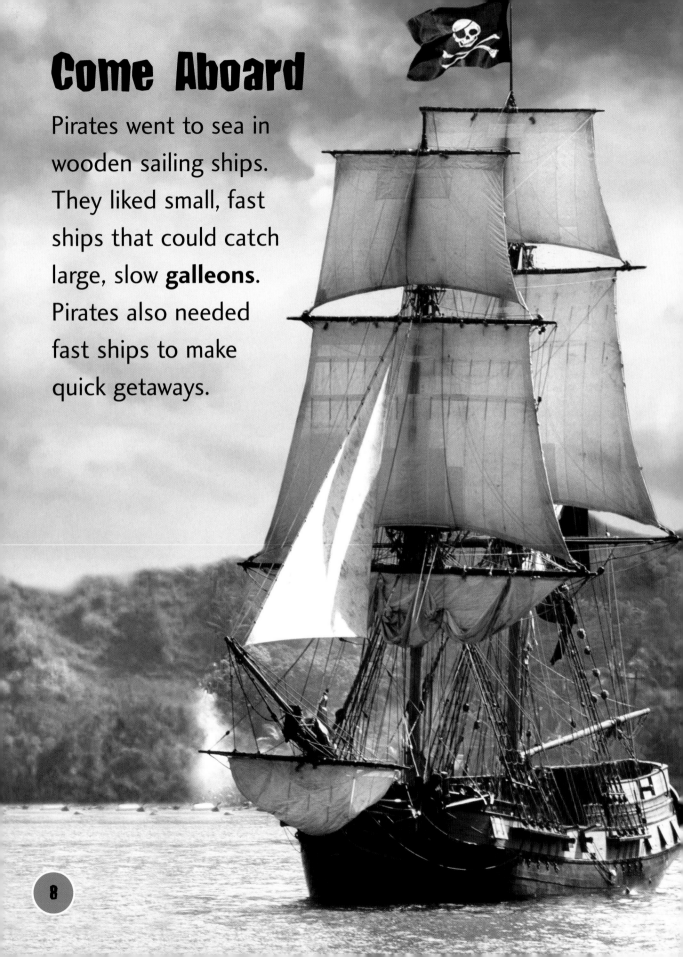

Come Aboard

Pirates went to sea in wooden sailing ships. They liked small, fast ships that could catch large, slow **galleons**. Pirates also needed fast ships to make quick getaways.

Sailing Ship Artifacts

Pirate ships were steered by a big wooden wheel that moved an underwater **rudder**.

At sea, a pirate crew had to work hard tugging on ropes to **set** the sails that drove the ship along. A pirate ship's top speed was about 17 miles (27 kilometers) per hour.

A compass showed the ship's captain which direction the ship was sailing.

A ship's huge, heavy anchor hooked into the seabed to hold the ship in one place.

Many pirate ships leaked! Underwater worms ate holes in the ships' wood bottoms.

Life on a Pirate Ship

Living at sea was dangerous. Some ships sank in storms, and everyone on board drowned. Pirates sometimes killed each other fighting over treasure. Sailors fell overboard, caught diseases, or starved when they ran out of food and fresh water.

On board ship, pirates usually ate **salt-meat** stews made by the ship's cook over a wood fire in the **galley**. The stew was eaten with hard, dry crackers that often had **maggots** wriggling inside. Sometimes, pirates got so hungry they cooked and ate their leather belts and shoes!

Living at sea was smelly, too. Nobody washed, the drinking water was usually bad, and the toilet was just a hole in the ship's deck, hanging over the sea.

On a pirate ship, only the captain had a private room, or cabin, for sleeping. The crew slept in **hammocks**, which they rolled up during the day.

Food and drinking water on pirate ships were stored in wooden barrels.

Pirates took chickens to sea with them for the eggs.

Many ships had goats that provided milk.

Pirate Weapons

Pirates looked fierce and carried lots of different weapons. When they attacked another ship, they fired guns, threw **grenades**, and slashed at people with cutlasses and **daggers**. Often, the crew on an attacked ship did not even try to fight back.

Pirate ships had big guns, called cannons, that fired huge, heavy balls made of iron.

Ships firing cannons in the movie *Pirates of the Caribbean: The Curse of the Black Pearl*.

A pirate's **flintlock pistol** took about thirty seconds to load and could fire only one shot at a time. Because the pistol needed reloading after each shot, a pirate carried five or six pistols with him during an attack.

Pirates used axes to chop through ropes and smash through cabin doors when they were searching for treasure.

A corsair.

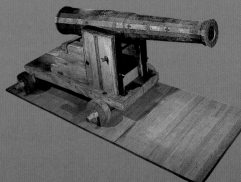

Cannons made a lot of noise and smoke, and they were hard to **aim**.

When they hit ships, cannonballs made showers of big wood splinters that were sharp enough to kill people.

A pirate's cutlass was short so it was easy to swing on a crowded deck.

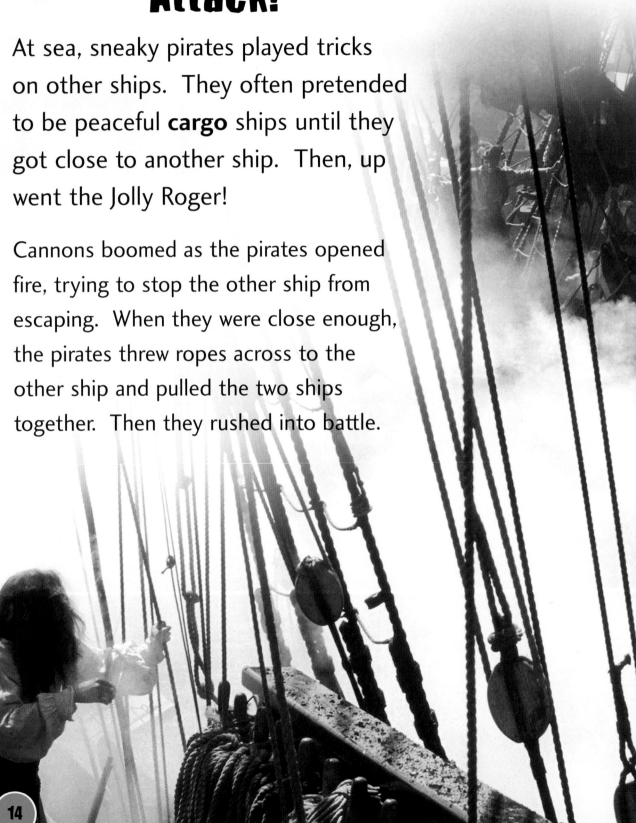

Attack!

At sea, sneaky pirates played tricks on other ships. They often pretended to be peaceful **cargo** ships until they got close to another ship. Then, up went the Jolly Roger!

Cannons boomed as the pirates opened fire, trying to stop the other ship from escaping. When they were close enough, the pirates threw ropes across to the other ship and pulled the two ships together. Then they rushed into battle.

Sometimes, pirates would sneak into a **port** at night and take over a ship while its crew slept.

A pirate attack from the movie *Pirates of the Caribbean: The Curse of the Black Pearl*.

Pirate Artifacts

When a grappling iron attached to a rope was thrown onto a ship under attack, its hooks held on tight to the ship's **rigging**.

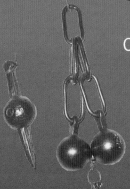

Chainshot fired by cannons smashed an attacked ship's **masts** and sails.

The pirate Blackbeard tied lighted gunpowder onto the ends of his hair to look extra scary in battle.

Pirate Treasure

When they attacked a ship, pirates hoped to find gold, silver, and jewels, but they also took silks, pearls, clothing, fresh food, weapons, and a ship's medicine chest.

Pirates would also steal a ship's ropes and sails to replace their own. Sometimes, the pirates even kept the captured ship if it was better than their own.

After an attack, pirates shared the treasure. The pirate captain always got the biggest share of the treasure. Pirate captain Bartholomew Roberts kept two shares, while his men got one share apiece.

Only pirates in stories buried their treasure on desert islands. Real pirates spent all their **loot** on having a good time.

Silver coins called "pieces of eight" could be cut into sections to be shared.

A ship's medicine chest was valuable because it contained medicines for treating diseases and battle wounds.

A gold **doubloon** was worth about seven weeks **wages** to a sailor.

17

Pirate Kingdoms

On land, pirates stayed in hideouts, where they could rest and have fun. The Caribbean and the Mediterranean were popular places for pirate hideouts. Where a lot of pirates were living together, no navy ship dared to attack.

North America

Europe

Mediterranean Sea

Atlantic Ocean

Africa

Port Royal

Caribbean Sea

South America

Port Royal, in Jamaica, was a famous pirate hideout. A Caribbean buccaneer named Henry Morgan led an army of pirates there.

KEEP OUT!

The Jolly Rogers on this map show the places where pirate hideouts could be found.

While on land, pirates had to repair and clean their ships. To clean **barnacles** and seaweed off of the bottom, or hull, of a ship, the ship was pulled onto its side in shallow water so that at least part of the hull was above water. Positioning a ship this way is called careening.

This bottle is three hundred years old. It contained wine or rum, both of which were popular pirate drinks.

Asia

South China Sea

Pacific Ocean

Indian Ocean

Australia

These playing cards came from a pirate ship. **Gambling** was one way a pirate quickly lost his share of a treasure!

Pirate Punishments

The punishment for piracy was death by hanging. A captured pirate could sometimes escape punishment by "telling" on his crewmates.

A pirate ship had rules. A pirate who broke the ship's rules might be left behind on a desert island to starve to death.

Pirate Ship Rules

No fighting with other crew members.

No candles or smoking near the cargo.

No stealing from crewmates.

Pirates put leg irons on their prisoners to keep them from running away.

Pirates could be very cruel to the sailors from the ships they captured, especially if they thought that the sailors had been cruel to pirates.

Some pirates carried out terrible punishments, such as cutting off a prisoner's lips and ears.

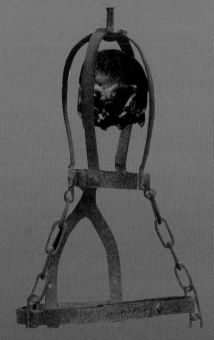

A hanged pirate's dead body was sometimes hung up in an iron cage as a warning to others.

A pirate who disobeyed his captain was beaten with a whip called a cat o' nine tails.

A World of Pirates

The Caribbean Sea was a favorite **haunt** for pirates, but they attacked ships all over the world. Cargo ships sailed along regular routes, so pirates always knew where to find them.

Mediterranean corsairs not only stole treasure but also kidnapped men they could use or sell as slaves. Corsairs went to sea in **galleys** that were rowed by slaves.

Corsairs in battle.

Buccaneers in the Caribbean attacked Spanish ships that were packed with gold from Mexico and Peru.

Chinese **junks** chased ships across the Indian Ocean and the South China Sea. Pirate king Ching-Chi-ling led a **fleet** of one thousand junks.

A model of a
Chinese junk.

When the salt-meat ran out
on pirate ships, the pirates
and their prisoners ate
rats with their rice.

In battle, galleys smashed
into the sides of other ships.

Asian pirates
fought with swords
that were decorated
with a lock of hair
from a dead enemy.

Glossary

aim: (v) to point at a target

ancient: from a time early in history

artifacts: items, such as tools and decorative objects, made by people

barnacles: small, hard-shelled sea animals that cling to boats and rocks

cargo: the goods carried on a ship

Caribbean: the sea that lies between North America and South America

cutlass: a short, often curved, sword

cutthroats: killers; murderers

daggers: short, double-edged knives

doubloon: an old Spanish gold coin

fleet: a group of ships controlled by the same person or organization

flintlock pistol: an old-time handgun that was packed with gunpowder to fire lead balls, instead of using bullets

galleons: large sailing ships with three masts and square sails

galley: a ship's kitchen; a ship that has both sails and oars

gambling: playing games for money

grenades: small bombs filled with gunpowder and usually thrown by hand

gruesome: horrible in a sickening way

hammocks: hanging beds made of rope or cloth

haunt: a place visited often

junks: Chinese ships with sails that look like slatted window shades

longships: very long sailing ships that had many oars along each side

loot: (n) stolen goods

maggots: small white worms that hatch from the eggs of houseflies

masts: the tall poles that hold a ship's rigging

merchant: related to selling or trading

navy: a country's warships

piracy: robbery on seas or oceans

port: a place where ships load and unload passengers and cargo

pregnant: carrying an unborn child

rigging: the ropes and chains that support the masts and sails on ships

rudder: a large, wide, flat piece of wood or metal that tilts from side to side to steer a boat or a ship

salt-meat: meat kept in salty water to make it last longer

set: (v) to lock into position

slaves: people who are captured and sold to work as servants

wages: money paid to a person in return for work